Scars and Stars

Kenneth Thompson

 FriesenPress

One Printers Way
Altona, MB R0G 0B0
Canada

www.friesenpress.com

ISBN
978-1-03-915981-5 (Hardcover)
978-1-03-915980-8 (Paperback)
978-1-03-915982-2 (eBook)

1. POETRY, SUBJECTS & THEMES, LOVE & EROTICA

Distributed to the trade by The Ingram Book Company

In all technical terms, these are poems.

First Dates

Our whole first date is planned out in my head
And it ends with us lying naked in my bed.
We'll go to the beach to swim in our birthday suits
Paying no mind to the people giving us disputes.
Every beach is a nudist beach if you break the law
Let these people see our bodies that lack any flaws.
Once we dry up we'll have a Taco Bell dinner
And whoever shits last will be declared the winner.
And to make sure we don't forget about romance
I'll take your hand and ask you to dance.
Do the waltz with me in the middle of the street
I apologize if I accidentally step on your feet.
Ignore the shouting people and honking cars
We'll pretend their headlights are actually stars.

Constellations

He didn't know how to be any more blunt
As she's always been at his brain's forefront
And though he still desired her touch
One could only admire so much.
He made a habit of growing bored quick
But wanted whatever they had to stick
Because if she took the chance to glance above her
She could even make the constellations love her.

The Calf and His Mother

The calf stood in the field next to his mother
With the grass and sky their only confines.
The breeze was cool and the land was vast
A feeling of serenity came to pass.
The mother looked at her darling
And felt her heart pang
For she knew this feeling was transient
And would end with a bang.
They would snatch him away soon
And butcher him for meat
So she said to look at the moon
As his one final treat.

Tattoos

Fuck the system and to hell with taboos
Her mind was reflected through her tattoos.
She saw her body through the prism of art
But nothing could cover the hurt in her heart.

Sins

Almost as if her heart has been split in half
She finds she cries just as much as she laughs.
They say finding happiness comes from within
Yet she found much more joy whenever she'd sin.

Denial

Her problems fled along with her fears
When he'd tuck her hair behind her ears.
Nothing can be fixed with a touch and smile
But how safe she felt hiding behind her denial.

Venice Beach

You say we'll experience joy and laughter soon
At this time tomorrow afternoon
Driving to Venice Beach for the day
Experiencing the view from the bay.
I picture you in your little high-waist shorts
With your stupid giggle and snorts
And my retorts about hating the beach and sand
Dissipate once I reach for your hand
And we're at the mercy of the waves underneath the pink sky
And I want to stay here with you until the ocean goes dry.

Jealous Fires

The splintering cold could freeze warm tears
To match these frozen toes and frost-bitten ears.
The biting breeze chills me to the core
With whistling winds impossible to ignore.
The snow drapes down like curtains on a rod
Our very lives feel at the mercy of a god.
Seems like this weather won't ever wither away
And the coldness and glumness are here to stay.
Even the fire shivers in the midst of this storm
I'm sure it's jealous you're here to keep me warm.

Bargains

I sold my soul to the devil since no one else was buying.
Suffice to say
It was a small price to pay
Since I never had a fear of dying.

Everything Feels Beautiful
and Nothing Hurts

Maybe he was meant to be alone in this world
Walking around feeling thrown and hurled
Feelings bounce off of him and only hit others
He leaves the moment he starts to feel smothered.
Yet a piece of his soul always begs him to stay
Since living in isolation comes with a pay
But he's smart enough to know he can't live in debt
So he's placing his money on one final bet.
He knows life is hollow when he emptily flirts
But everything feels beautiful and nothing hurts.

Worlds

The shape of your body and the scent of your hair
Is imprinted in my pillow and is permanently there.
Clothes tossed on the floor without a single care
You can draw me in with just a stare.
Care not for the light steeping in from the blinds
We're just two hearts beating with similar minds
Hands clasped together with fingers intertwined
Entering our world to leave all the rest behind.

Souls

Eyes are the windows to a person's soul
But souls need privacy too.
Everyone's always up in their business
As if they don't have their own personal affairs.
What if someone walked in on my soul
Making out with someone else's soul?
Does my soul get more action than I do?
Or maybe my soul just wants some alone time
And you're over here trying to force eye contact.
Chill out dude.
Let my soul live without the judgment.
What if souls aren't even real
And we're staring into nothing?
I guess staring into eyes isn't nothing
Because even if you can't see into my soul
At the very least you'll see me.

KENNETH THOMPSON

Sleep

It's not like we talk so I'm sure you're unaware
I dislike sleeping since I know you'll be there
Avoiding you in reality but adoring you in dreams
You make life more beautiful than it actually seems.

Fine

You do all you can to make him care
Though the odds are fairly slim there.
All the feelings you dared not speak about
Suddenly burst, rupture, and leak out.
You tell him 'I'm fine' time and time again
Knowing this is the typical crime of men
But you'd confess it all if he were to just ask it
You'd snuggle up next to him as he lay in his casket.
If only he were to ask if you were truly fine
You would say that you were
Just as long as you're mine.

Recurring Dreams

Every night I have the same three recurring dreams.
The first starts off rather cliché
I'm a child swinging on a beautiful day.
My feet point towards the sky
With my father pushing me from behind.
I take no heed of the honking cars
The hustle-bustle of the city fades away.
But then suddenly my momentum starts to slow
And my father is no longer behind me
And I stare back into his absence.
Thinking he is playing a game with me
I search for him behind the shed
Behind the small aboveground pool
Behind the one large tree we have in the backyard.
Starting to feel worried
I express my concern by welling up.
I say his name but he does not answer.
Though I am the one looking for him
I am the one who feels lost in my own backyard.
I cannot find him
And I say his name
And he is not there
And then I wake up.

The second dream is just as cliché
I'm driving on an empty road on another sunny day.
In a convertible speeding down a winding road
Its trail outlining a mountain I don't know the name of.
It's leading to the very top
Which I assume has an exciting destination
Though in this dream I never know what it is.
That's not the point of it
I know that
But when I wake up I cannot help but wonder.
I cannot help but wonder where I'm driving to
Where I so badly want to escape
Or what I so badly want to find.
I drive contently with no one in my passenger seat
It is empty with the potential for a new friend.
Perhaps I meet this new friend on the way to the top
Or perhaps I meet them later in life.
Either way it is waiting for them
And I continue driving until I reach the top
But I don't ever reach the top.
The winding road winds a bit too sharply
And I find myself losing control
But before I regain what little control I had
I find myself going off of the cliff
And I catch a whiff of the life I led.
Everything flashes across my mind
But before the mental relapse of my life is played
I wake up next to some woman that I paid.

KENNETH THOMPSON

The third dream
Well
The third dream is so close and personal to me
That perhaps it's best it stays a dream.

Vague

My love for you is as sweet as honey.
You're a lot like my aunt
But younger and not mean and I don't owe you money.
I'll keep your characteristics vague so that I don't out you
But just know I love everything about you.
For example
I love your vague smile
And your vague hair
And your vague eyes.
Not to mention that vague thing you do
That makes me think how much I love you.
I will love you until you're an old dwindling greying hag
Even then my love will be so strong yet so very, very vague.

KENNETH THOMPSON

Just in Case

Forgetting the people I made room in my heart for
I'm now super fucking cool and chill and hardcore.
Yet if I'm being honest there's still a bit of space
With the exact proportions of your size and face
Because even if the odds are slim or none at all
It's nice to leave a bit of room just in case.

Bed

She always had her bed to escape to
After those days where she'd barely scrape through
But she feels it's been tainted now that he's not there
So her bed feels like yet another place that isn't fair.
What was once a haven where they'd cuddle for years
Has now been reduced to a puddle of tears
With the empty pillow next to her calling his name
But she's tried that already and he never came.

Clear Nights

Summer came quickly and singing birds filled the air
Bummer he's been finding it hard to show that he cares.
When a clear night appears with the moon floating above
He's certain that's the closest he'll get to experience love.

Day Dreams

As strange as it may seem
I've never been one to daydream.
I save these thoughts for late at night
For when I can play things out just right.
These thoughts usually consist of you and me
Confined to my mind is when I feel most free.

Pride

Her solution to fixing what was broken
Was to leave her words left unspoken.
Best to keep it bottled up inside
Because if she couldn't protect her feelings
She'd at least protect her pride.

A Poker Player Bluffing
Her Way to Victory

She was hard to read
But that's what made her so attractive.
She was like a poker player bluffing her way to victory.
She couldn't be tricked or thieved
For she had her own tricks up her sleeves.
They thought her clever and conniving and cunning
Her piercing dark eyes were absolutely stunning
A smile that expressed more words than you or I
An attitude that only knew do or die
A frame built frail but a heart made of stone
A game she couldn't fail even when played on her own.
She was the perfect person to fall in love with
Someone you'd only hear about in myths
But you know she's too smart for someone like you
She's as opaque as you are see-through
But you carry on since you have her now
Even though you truly don't know how
You continue living as if you deserve this
With her feelings fleeing faster than your first kiss.

Bob

I once had a cat named Bob
Who contributed little to the household
So I made him get a job.
Next thing I know
He's raking in dough
Now I'm paying rent to Bob.

Planets

I never thought much of our future
I've yet to really plan it.
We could move to Paris or New York
Or an entirely different planet.
Jupiter or Neptune or Saturn or Mars
We can even attempt to terraform stars.
But just for now this planet will do
It shines so bright all thanks to you.

KENNETH THOMPSON

Reminder

She's as confident as she is insecure
She's as deviant as she is pure.
She's a lot like me only a little bit more
She makes me remember what a heart is for.

Short and Sweet

Don't have long so I'll keep it short and sweet
The days we don't speak feel a bit incomplete
And I think I can testify on everyone's behalf
There's no better feeling than making you laugh.

Literate

I'm shit at hellos and worse at goodbyes
Our world went to shit and I just stood by.
The times I've let my feelings bleed through
Are the times I've found it difficult to read you.
I thought I was literate but maybe I'm wrong
I can't help but think of you no matter the song.

Beautiful Worlds

They say the world is beautiful yet here we are
Avoiding what's around us by staring at the stars.
We say the world is beautiful in an effort to get by
But our world could be beautiful with just you and I.

Recurring Dreams II

I'm reminded of the third dream when doing mundane tasks.
Reading a book on the subway
Watering my wilting plant on my balcony
Drying dishes.
In the dream I am doing all these boring chores
The only difference is you're there with me.
They feel more like memories than they do dreams
Floating through my mind like a log down a stream.
Perhaps it's because they were once the truth
With me and you living boringly together
Thinking we would be like this forever.
I live my life waiting for someone–
Anyone who looks like they have authority over my life–
To tell me that what I dream no longer needs to stay a dream.
We can go back to the life we shared
And neither of us needs to wake up sad again.

Garden

I should be happy sitting in this garden
Instead of feeling my heart harden.
Like the roses stemming from the ground
I tend to root myself in whoever is around
Only to be forcibly plucked from the dirt
And I'm meant to act like it never even hurt.

Anchors

She wished she could find comfort at an alter
Each time she felt her feelings falter.
Or be the type that goes for a run
Anytime she feels she's emotionally done.
Or open a book when she's feeling down
Or socialize with friends when they hit up the town.
But there's an anchor within her that's been born
As if she was made to perpetually mourn.
It weighs her down and pins her to her bed
Forcing her to lie with the thoughts in her head.
She doesn't quite recall all they've said
But it was something about wishing she were dead.
Anchors are heavy and so is her heart
At the very least she'll make beautiful art.

Happily Ever After

The world will catch fire one of these days
And everyone alive will go down in a blaze
With her last words being nothing but laughter
Since death, for her, meant happily ever after.

Heartbeat

I feel your rapid pulse and heartbeat
And my initial impulse is to retreat
Because fleeing is easier than feeling
And like hell I'll be caught kneeling
But my heart has a mind of its own
And it prefers you over being alone.

Sweat Glands

Pardon my wet hands
It's these damn overactive sweat glands
Kicking into overdrive when you're around
And I feel like my body has all but drowned.
In order to survive I cling to what's near
So luckily for me I have you here
But if you'd like we can just drown holding hands
Sinking in the sweat of my overactive sweat glands.

Odds Are

We have a better shot at meeting the gods
Than we do of beating the odds.
If we haven't happened yet I doubt we ever will
But I suppose if I had to I would die on this hill.
Why not join me since it's got a lovely view
We can mark the occasion I fell in love with you.

Thirty Millions Memories

We'll go for a walk and roam together
Then afterwards chill at home together.
Whether it be your bed or mine
My finger will trace your body's outline
And we'll fall asleep knowing when we wake
There'll be thirty million more memories to make.

This Is My Attempt At Writing A Rupi-Kaur-Style Poem. I Have Not Read Anything By Her So This May Be An Inaccurate Depiction But Enjoy This Poem Nonetheless

Love is a wilting flower waiting for its gardener to come.

She never comes.

She's Such A Happy Girl

She's such a happy girl
She cries each time she drinks beer.
Or at least she thinks it's happiness
She tends not to think very clear.
She acts as messy as the way that she feels
Walking like she's got one broken heel
Running mascara and knotted hair
Tumbling as she makes it up the stairs
Bent over the toilet with her hair pulled back
Crying over some boy named Ryan or Zach.

She's such a happy girl
She cries each time she drinks beer.
Or at least she thinks it's happiness
Either way she's reduced to tears.
Her friends call him a monster
But she sees no scales or claws
Just a boy with a few too many flaws.
She sends him that late night text
With no response rendering her perplexed.
One more shot and that'll do the trick
It'll all be worth it when she wakes up sick.

KENNETH THOMPSON

She's such a happy girl
She cries each time she drinks beer.
Or at least she thinks it's happiness
She knows she's avoiding her fears.
Her soul mate is waiting for her at the bar
Hooking up in the back of a car
She doesn't quite know it yet
But he's being added to her list of regrets.
Part of her thinks she loves it
For love is all she covets.

She's such a happy girl
She cries each time she drinks beer.
Or at least she think it's happiness
Reality is growing near.
Flirting with men she knows are taken
Her own feelings are too much to take in
So she goes and manipulates others
Then leaves when she starts to feel smothered.
She's such a happy girl
Yet she cries each time she drinks beer.

Insecurities

Whatever insecurities you feel
I wouldn't attempt to fix or heal
The parts of you that you try to conceal
Are the parts perfection wishes to steal.

We Go Together

We go together like brains and tumors
We go together like pain and humor.
An insane rumor has been going around
Saying you're lost looking to be found.
I may be just the guy to guide you
I'm quite familiar with wanting to hide too.
Stored away inside of my head
Bored days inside of my bed.
I suspect you know precisely how this feels
Sedentary when thoughts are spinning like wheels.
Only comfort comes from the possibility of change
A table for two can easily be arranged.

Megaphones

If I had a megaphone to shout through
You could've heard how I talked about you.
Now my mouth is shut but my mind is racing
Trying to process the change we're facing.
When I think of you my heart still goes warm
Even if us not speaking has become the norm.

Better Late Than Never

She couldn't get all she wanted by being clever
A realization that was better late than never.
It only took her a few too many years to learn
That love is only excellent if you get it in return.

Habits

Life goes on but the habits rarely change
She's a tad fucked up and super fucking strange.
Rearranging the pieces that don't quite fit
Avoiding the truths she's too scared to admit.
She found her independence but at what cost?
No amount of wins can undo all that she's lost.

Time

Time creeps forward with no end in sight
The thought of death does tend to fright.
On her final days she intends to write
Questioning how her life has descended to plight.
Repenting for the time spent with her head in a book
Unrelenting curiosity had grasped her with its hooks.
Now look at where that inquisition has gotten her
The loved ones she has left have all but forgotten her.
Time creeps forward as if it's got a curfew
The hours she's spent alone are more than just a few.
If time teaches anything it's that it's as long as it is short
Dying by ones self should only come as a last resort.

Blushing Skies

Staying up late 'til we meet the sunrise
Awakening to you is always a surprise.
Turning to see your lovely little head
You make the sky blush a beautiful red.

Moments of Pleasure

Why do moments of pleasure only last a moment?
She'd prefer it if they'd last a few more seconds
Or perhaps a full minute
Because how sweet is that moment once you're in it?
Maybe it'd be best to block those thoughts out
But there was nothing she'd rather think about
Than remembering those happy moments they had
Only for them to be the source of why she's so sad.

Fires

Falling for him was as easy as igniting a fire in hell
Perhaps one day he'll fall in love with her as well.

Piece of Art

I thought I was so clever and funny and smart
And no one could compete with my wit and art
But the art I love most isn't one I could create
Since it looks like you on our very first date.

House

Dinner was ready and the table was candlelit
Pressure was on but he figured he'd handle it.
Alone in this house as it croaks and creeks
Finishing in bed as he strokes her cheek.
These four little walls are all they've had
He never knew beautiful could look so sad.

First is First

She tended to want things she never had
Which is why she wanted to be loved so bad.
Alone in her bed thinking she's been cursed
But love finds those who find themselves first.

High Beams

He could've sworn the light was green
He got distracted by the text on his screen.
Blinded by the pair of oncoming high beams
He hardly had time to let out a scream.
Just enough time to see his loved ones faces
He managed to find some kind of oasis.
A particular image flashed across his mind
Remembering what he'd be leaving behind.

He first saw his two beautiful daughters
Gleefully playing on their favorite teeter-totter.
Then came his son coming down the slide
His head held high beaming with pride.
His wife watched as they played their games
That beautiful way she'd adjust her frames.
He really could've sworn that the light was green
'Pick something up for dinner' stayed lit on the screen.

Sleeping Pills

Taking a sleeping pill to go to bed
She entered a whole new world in her head.
One that existed of only her and him
With his absence weighing like a phantom limb.
Wishing to escape from reality and how she feels
Her dreams hurt more than if they were real.

In Sync

Maybe one day their heart rates will be in sync
And they'll care not for what others think
But for now they're left with no future or past
Endlessly entering relationships that do not last.
The thing no one mentions about having a broken heart
Is it's difficult to break when it's been empty from the start.

Demons

Sunny days always made the pain stop
Up until she felt the first few raindrops.
In this mood it would take awhile
Just for him to make her smile.
Fortunately he was clever and cunning
And he could send her demons running
So if you wanted to say he loved her wildly
Well
Let's just say that'd be putting it mildly.

Drinks

After a drink or two or three
I tend to think of you and me.
Ditching parties early to go walk and wander
I find alcohol makes the heart grow fonder.
Not normally this sappy but we'll blame the wine
I'm just happy your feelings are the same as mine.

KENNETH THOMPSON

Weather

Roses bloom at the scent of your perfume
Birds sing as loud as church bells ring
Tides compete to wash over your feet
Winds catch speed to fulfill your every need.
Nature fights to create the perfect weather
All so we can enjoy our time together.

Taxes

Okay look
This may sound shocking to you
But I really dislike not talking to you.
I also dislike being all sappy and heartfelt
But one look at you can make my heart melt.
Poetry is lame unless it's coming from me
I tax others for my feelings but for you they're free.

In Awe

The mirror is cursed with the image of you
Reflecting what you always knew to be true
But if you asked the mirror what it saw
It, like me, would just stare at you in awe.

City of Thousands

Looking up to see her dark eyes and light hair
He instantly knew they'd make the right pair.
He'd yet to see someone so irrefutably fair
As he saw her laughing beautifully there.
His feelings for others had always been fairly rare
He'd flirt and have sex and would still barely care
He knew love to be an emotion that was rarely fair
Yet he approached this one with a warily air.
It wasn't often he felt his heart flutter rapidly
He felt a fool when he'd speak and stutter vapidly
Yet there was a simple message he wanted to get out
One that would put an end to all her doubts.
Whatever they lacked in immediate connection
He'd be sure to make up for in genuine affection.
They would make it work and if they'd regret it
Then they'd mutually agree to just forget it.
He figured it'd be a pity if that were the case
City of thousands but he only saw her face.

KENNETH THOMPSON

Alphabet

The alphabet contains all the things I'd say to you
The perfect conflation of letters that'd make life better.
Twenty-six symbols could be the fix
Or just a few would do the trick.
I could sing them or write them or say them aloud
I'll scream through a megaphone into a crowd.
If that's too much then I understand
I have other techniques that are perfectly planned.
I'll whisper them to you to be discreet
Whatever we have is just our little treat.
The way that I tell you matters not
I just know a few dozen feelings have been caught.

Beautiful Mind

There wasn't anything wrong per se
But she felt nothing was going her way.
Empty feelings would pass her by
Going unchecked by every passerby
But open her heart and take pliers to her brain
To find happiness and love infused with pain
But look even further and you'll likely find
The recipe for the utmost beautiful mind.

Dreams

The scariest thing about nightmares
Is their tendency to come true.
Not the ones where I'm being mauled by a bear
Or where I'm in public wearing only underwear
But the ones where you are you
And I am me
But we aren't together for all to see.
That kind of sucks since they're actually true
Yet another night where I'm dreaming of you.

Oceans

Though I love you in that sundress
It may be best if we undress
Since waves hit differently in the nude
Our bodies can serve the ocean like food.
The only mystery lying beneath the sea
Is the one that looks like you and me
With the ocean waves matching the blue skies
Yet no ocean can compete with your blue eyes.

KENNETH THOMPSON

Starlit Skies

I could write you crappy poetry all day and night
And you can act as if you like it to seem polite
But in the end there's only one thing I know to be true
The starlit skies are painfully beautiful
Even if they're only half as pretty as you.

Mood Swings

Her mood swings like a pendulum back and forth
Since she isn't quite certain of what she is worth
So her reaction may vary depending on the day
A busy mind with a mouth not knowing what to say.

KENNETH THOMPSON

Room

Bookshelf creaks with the knowledge it supports
Towel clings to life as it hangs on the door
Clothes on the floor with a desk collecting dust
Hinges on the window covered in rust.
What a decrepit room we find ourselves in
Unwashed bed sheets that are well worn thin
The curtains are stained with God-knows-what
The walls have cracks like veins on a hand
And this sorry excuse of a three-legged nightstand.
We pay all this no heed as we lay on this mattress
Our overlapping body and our hair a mess
Talking beneath the moon then sleeping 'til noon
Happily feeling high and listening to tunes.
We open the window and we hear the tide
Along with birds chirping cheerily outside.
If you look up you'll see the crumbling ceiling
And beneath are two people in love with this feeling.

Scars and Stars

Whoever it is you think you are
I know we both carry similar scars
Which is why our humor goes too far
Let me see those eyes that resemble stars.

KENNETH THOMPSON

Holy Shit

Holy shit
How much harder does she need to try
Before finishing a day without wanting to cry?
Does she blame capitalism or psychology or just bad luck?
Does she game the system by not giving a fuck?
There's no solution because the problem isn't even clear
The world is ending but it feels like death is already here.

Self-Destruction

She's meant to be funny and charming and witty, right?
Even after having yet another shitty night?
Love won't save her but perhaps pity might
She makes self-destruction look like such a pretty sight.

Setting Suns

Eyes are dark with hair light like the sun
One look at you can make me feel undone.
My heart pounds as fast as this sun sets
And the closer you are to it
The prettier it gets.

Responsibilities

She drives back home and cherishes her sleep
To avoid responsibilities she swore she'd keep
But life somehow follows her into her dreams
Filling the room with the quietest of screams.

Similarities

I spot the similarities between you and me
So I know you well to a varying degree.
You get called beautiful and know it to be true
But everyone's got it all wrong
Since beautiful should ask to be you.

Poses

She thought they'd take pretty pictures with poses
By daisies and roses
With kisses on noses
And when the day closes
They'd settle down with a glass of wine
With fingers made to intertwine.
Instead this happened only in her head
With her heart feeling as empty as her bed.

KENNETH THOMPSON

Lunatic

Anyone anywhere could easily fall for you
Since I can see why they'd all adore you
But admiration of beauty only goes so far
So I promise to dig you for who you are
Which is a crazy lunatic disguised as sanity
But I'd quickly pick you over all of humanity.

Insomnia

I write of dreams as if I have any
As if I am not held hostage by insomnia.
On the rare occasion my eyelids droop
And I am whisked away into a tenuous slumber
I still find my dreams to be void of meaning.
I am confronted with facts I already know to be true
Because these facts reveal themselves to me while I'm awake.
I understand everything there is to know.
I know that death is possible without dying
Because you cannot experience death when you're dead
Because, well, you're dead.
I find no comfort in the supernatural
Because the burden on gods shoulders means one thing
And that one thing is that the dude must be under some serious stress.
If this is true
And god cannot find happiness
Then I suppose all humans are screwed
Because if god can't find happiness then how can you?
My insomnia makes me confront questions I cannot answer
With my mind racing in a track meet I was not equipped to run.
My dreams are void of laughter and fun
Because they are littered with past events
That brings me shame and regret and heartbreak
So perhaps insomnia isn't so bad after all
Because when I dream I must confront my past
But when I am awake I can create futures that won't ever come true.

KENNETH THOMPSON

Though this thought may be sad
I cling to it knowing that maybe I am wrong
And the visions I have in my dreams were false all along.

Literacy

If it's written in the stars then I can't fucking read
I keep getting what I want but not what I need.
If the stars are writing anything then I must be blind
The only peaceful world that exists is inside my mind.

Nightmares

I have this dream where you're standing right there
And it quickly descends into a nightmare
Because even though I see you
You stare at me like I'm see through
And everything I was afraid we would ever be
Becomes real when I realize there's no more you and me.

Bluest of Blue

He figured they would end up together
He just didn't know how or when
It was just a thought he had every now and then.
Sitting together as his mind went adrift
Picturing what could be her next gift
With the garden underneath them being a solid clue
He'd search for flowers that were the bluest of blue.

Ending Poem

After everything I've wrote
It'd be good to end on a high note
Yet I'm left with all that I feel
For my nightmares only ever become real
But if I refrain from sleeping by staying awake
Then I will never need to confront my every mistake
And I can pretend to be happy to please those around me
While ignoring the dark thoughts that tend to surround me
So why not join me with this foolproof plan
Because I cannot do this alone
But perhaps together we can.

Instagram: @technicallypoems

TikTok: @technicallypoems

Feel free to follow me in person, too. I've always wanted a stalker.

Lightning Source UK Ltd.
Milton Keynes UK
UKHW040943160223
417122UK00002B/377

9 781039 159808